WORLD HISTORY

Early River Civilizations

WORLD
HISTORY

World History: Early River Civilizations

Copyright © 2011 by Morgan Reynolds Publishing

Library of Congress Cataloging-in-Publication Data

Nardo, Don, 1947-
Early river civilizations / by Don Nardo. -- 1st ed.
   p. cm. -- (World history)
Includes bibliographical references and index.
ISBN 978-1-59935-140-7
1. Civilization, Ancient--Juvenile literature. 2.
Rivers--History--Juvenile literature. 3. River life--History--Juvenile
literature. I. Title.
CB311.N28 2010
930.1--dc22

                                    2010008693

Printed in the United States of America
First Edition

Book cover and interior designed by:
Ed Morgan, navyblue design studio
Greensboro, NC

WORLD HISTORY

EARLY RIVER CIVILIZATIONS

Dan Nardo

GREENSBORO, NORTH CAROLINA

Pyramids at Gizeh with dhows on the Nile River

Table of Contents

Chapter One:
The Land Between the Rivers

"Rivers must have been the guides which conducted the footsteps of the first travelers. They are the constant lure . . . to distant enterprise and adventure, [and] they are the natural highways of all nations." So wrote the noted American writer Henry David Thoreau in the nineteenth century.

Like many other modern thinkers and scholars, Thoreau recognized that rivers have long played a key role in spreading and nurturing human civilization. The earliest humans not only went to riverbanks to drink—they were hunter-gatherers, and they saw that many of the animals they killed for food also relied on rivers for water. So the river valleys often attracted nomadic bands of people who could count on bountiful hunts in those regions.

Later, after some human groups discovered agriculture, the rivers became attractive in a different way. The soil near the riverbanks was rich and supported all manner of crops. Also, the rivers supplied the abundant water needed to irrigate those crops. This potent combination of fertile soil and plentiful water led to large-scale farming. Extensive, reliable, and permanent farms facilitated the growth of large permanent settlements. Over time, these communities grew into the first cities and nations.

In this way, rivers proved key factors in the emergence of the earliest major civilizations. Historians recognize four so-called cradles of human civilization, each of which developed along the banks of one or more large rivers. In Mesopotamia, what is now Iraq, the life-giving rivers were the Tigris and Euphrates. (The term *Mesopotamia* comes from Greek words meaning "the land between the rivers.") Egyptian civilization thrived on the banks of the Nile, in northeastern Africa; the Yellow River supported the rise of a great civilization in China; and India's Indus River made possible the hundreds of cities and settlements built by the Harappan people.

Modern-day map of what was once Mesopotamia

Of these ancient cultural centers, Mesopotamia was the pioneer. Its inhabitants were the first both to exploit large-scale farming and to build cities and city-states. The residents of the Nile, Yellow, and Indus valleys later repeated many of the steps taken by the early peoples of the Tigris-Euphrates valley.

From Small- to Large-Scale Farming

The first step in the long process that led to the earliest cities was the emergence of agriculture. Initially, progress occurred on a very small scale. The world's first known farms sprang up in the low hills lying north and west of the Mesopotamian river plains. The area stretched in an arc from Palestine and Syria, through southeastern Anatolia (now Turkey), across Iraq's northern rim, and into northern Iran. Scholars call this region of ample rains and rich soils the Fertile Crescent. About 9000 BC (11,000 years ago), its inhabitants learned to grow crops, such as wheat, barley, peas, lentils, cucumbers, lettuce, apples, and grapes. People made a thick porridge out of the barley, and they combined barley with wheat to make a nutritious flat bread. In addition, they raised domesticated animals, including sheep, cattle, goats, pigs, ducks, and oxen (used to pull plows).

These plants and animals proved to be stable, dependable food sources for the people of the Fertile Crescent. With a constant supply of food, they could remain in one area rather than roam far and wide to hunt and gather. Now that they stayed in the same place, they needed permanent shelters. So they erected small settlements—the first villages. Modern scholars estimate that each village had between ten and thirty crude huts, which were typically made of thatch (bundled tree branches) or mud-bricks. Archaeologists have found the remains of a few of these tiny settlements, including one at Qalat Jarmo, just north of the Tigris-Euphrates valley.

Over the centuries, these tiny settlements expanded somewhat in population. By about 5500 BC some of the residents of the Fertile Crescent began migrating southward onto the plains. "People may have perceived that their villages were getting too crowded," writes University of Oklahoma historian Daniel C. Snell, "even if they may not have been crowded at all by later standards. And so they moved out into the forbid-

Domesticating Plants and Animals

One of the main achievements of the agricultural revolution in the Fertile Crescent was the taming of certain key plants and animals, as pointed out by noted historian and writer L. Sprague de Camp:

> The Agricultural Revolution, which made village life both possible and compulsory, probably began in this mountainous arc because here dwelt the beasts and plants that . . . proved the easiest and most useful to tame. These are the ox, the goat, the sheep, the pig, and the grasses wheat and barley. There are, of course, many other useful plants and animals. . . . [Later, people] domesticated such plants as rice, maize [corn], and other fruits and vegetables. [But] other species did not turn out well and were abandoned. Most of the food that [people] consume today is still derived from wheat, rice, and maize, and from the ox, the goat, the sheep, and the pig.

ding frontier area, which turned out to be extremely productive agriculturally."

The river valley offered these immigrants chances for expansion they had never dreamed possible. They now had seemingly endless supplies of water for irrigation. Also, the rivers periodically deposited fresh layers of fertile soil near their banks, which could be used to enrich the earth; this also prevented the farmland from becoming arid or strained from overproduction.

Not only did farming suddenly become much larger in scope, it stimulated the emergence of new and more diverse labor skills, social groups, and institutions. The widely respected historian W. H. McNeill, who has written numerous books about how civilizations develop, explains:

Once the feasibility of growing crops with an artificial water supply had been demonstrated, agricultural settlement in the great desert valleys of the Tigris-Euphrates opened a new range of possibilities to pioneer communities. . . . The new environment was strikingly different from the hill country, where farming had first begun. The rivers with their tangle of swamps and bayous made fishing . . . an important activity. [The] riches of the river valley gave rise to a comparatively dense population [and] diverging interests and outlook of fishers, herdsmen, and cultivators, all of whom had to live [together]. Such conditions called for larger social units [and] it became possible for relatively dense populations to sustain life. . . . The presence of such large populations in turn provided the [mass] labor power needed for erecting monumental [large-scale] structures, for extending the system of dykes and canals to new ground year by year, and for performing the tasks of long-distance transport [i.e., trade] required by the growing complexity of their style of life.

Ubaidians and Sumerians

Large-scale food production along the rivers led to the emergence of towns. These communities had populations of a thousand and sometimes as many as 2,000 or more residents, compared to the mere hundred or so inhabitants in the upland farming villages. Among these new towns were Choga Mami and Tepe Gawra in northern Mesopotamia. Further south, near the Persian Gulf, were Eridu, Uruk, Ur, and Tell al-Ubaid. Historians call the early inhabitants of these communities Ubaidians (named for Tell al-Ubaid).

The Ubaidians maintained a thriving culture along the rivers for at least fifteen centuries. (Modern scholars call the years from circa 5000 to 3500 BC Mesopotamia's Ubaidian period.) Almost nothing is known about Ubaidian society and customs, but recent excavations reveal some facts about the towns themselves. Each featured not only houses and shops made of mud-bricks, but also a few larger buildings. These larger buildings were likely used as granaries for grain storage, as well as religious temples for worship. In his Historical Atlas of Ancient Mesopotamia, Norman B. Hunt describes the structures in the town of Eridu:

> By the close of the Ubaid[ian] period, [an earthen] mound at Eridu had become a raised platform that was reached by a flight of steps. On its summit stood a complex temple . . . which contained an altar surrounded by a series of subsidiary rooms. Surrounding the earth mound were elaborate homes, presumed to belong to a social elite, and craft workshops beyond these. Farmers' houses were on the outskirts of [town], with irrigated fields farther out.

The next major change in the region occurred in the mid-to-late 3000s BC. A people now called the Sumerians settled the flat, lush lands lying northwest of the Persian Gulf. The area, encompassing most of southern Mesopotamia, became known as Sumer. (Actually, Sumer is the name for the region given centuries later by the Babylonians. The Sumerians themselves called it Kengir, which meant "civilized land.") Exactly who the Sumerians were and where they came from is unknown. They may have been Ubaidians who had become more culturally advanced and migrated. Or they may have been foreigners who entered Mesopotamia from the east.

Wherever they came from, the Sumerians dominated the area for more than a thousand years. They created an advanced culture that profoundly influenced later Mesopotamian and Middle Eastern peoples. One contribution they made was the first sophisticated writing system, which peoples in the region later adopted. Dubbed cuneiform, it used little wedge-shape marks to stand for words, objects, and concepts. The marks were made on moist clay tablets that, when hardened, became the first permanent books and written records.

Cuneiform Writing

One of the Sumerians' major gifts to human civilization was the cuneiform writing system. The word *cuneiform* comes from the Latin term *cuneus*, meaning "wedge." Cuneiform markings are wedge-shaped and were most often pressed onto clay tablets. Such writing allowed people to keep detailed inventories of goods and financial records. It also gave them the ability to create law codes, personal letters, medical treatises, historical accounts, written prayers, and works of literature. The most famous Sumerian literary work was the *Epic of Gilgamesh*. Its 3,500 lines of text told the story of a man who tried to find the secret of immortality, but failed. Later Mesopotamian peoples, including the Babylonians and Assyrians, adopted cuneiform to their own languages.

The Sumerian religion also served as a model for other peoples later inhabiting the region, including the Babylonians and Assyrians. Religion affected many aspects of Sumerian life. People believed that a large number of gods and other invisible spirits existed. These beings supposedly guided human activities, including growing crops, healing the sick, and making war. It was also thought that the gods made strict rules of order that humans were supposed to follow. The Sumerians called these rules me. (Later, the Babylonians and Assyrians called them parsu.)

Another aspect of their religion that shaped daily life was worship. People regularly prayed to the gods, a practice conducted privately or under the leadership of priests who held public worship at temples in the towns and cities. Certain gods were seen as protectors of specific groups. For example, soldiers prayed to deities thought to watch over military men, and farmers prayed to patron gods of the fields and fertility. Individual towns also had patron deities, who, it was believed, took a particular interest in those communities.

The rise of Assyria brought into prominence the national god Assur, shown here, who was also the city god of Assur, the ancient capital.

As religious beliefs and worship passed from generation to generation, they became ingrained in society. They contributed to a strong sense of morality and community among the Sumerians, and later among peoples across Mesopotamia.

The First Cities

Still another important cultural contribution made by the Sumerians was the introduction of the world's first cities, which began to emerge in the late 3000s BC. What made them cities becomes evident when one compares them to the Ubaidian towns that preceded them. A typical town of that era covered between ten and twenty acres and had about one thousand residents. Uruk, for instance, lying a few miles northwest of Ur, at some time in the 4000s BC qualified as such a town.

But by 3500–3400 BC Uruk had far surpassed any town in both size and population. With about two hundred acres and 10,000 inhabitants, it had grown to become the first true city, or urban center, in Mesopotamia, or anywhere else. And it continued to grow apace. By the mid-2000s BC it spanned 1,200 acres (almost two square miles) and had a population of more than 50,000. Several other Sumerian cities became almost as large, including Lagash, Ur, Kish, Umma, Sippar, and Nippur, among others.

It was not merely the size of these communities that made them cities; it was also the complexity of their life and the diversity of their buildings, institutions, and occupations. Moreover, cities were protected around the perimeter by massive walls and other defenses. As the late historian Chester G. Starr put it:

> Each city proper was girdled by a moat and
> wall of sun-dried brick; that of Uruk eventually
> stretched almost 6 miles, with over 900 towers.
> . . . [Inside] the gates . . . streets wide enough
> for chariots and wagons ran between blocks of

The Jordan River. With a steady stream of bleak predictions that "water wars" will be fought over dwindling supplies in the twenty-first century, battles between two Sumerian city-states 4,500 years ago seem to have set a worrying precedent.

houses of the well-to-do. Behind these were
alleys and great masses of small, flat-roofed huts.
Here lived mostly the farmers, who trudged out
every day to the fields. . . . But there were also
[metal]smiths, potters, and [other craftsmen].
Looming over the homes of men were the temples, very literally conceived as the "houses of
the gods."

Outside the defensive walls, as Starr alludes to, stretched
vast fields where farmers cultivated food to support the city.
Complex networks of irrigation canals criss-crossed the fields.
These waterways were connected to and supplied by the near-
est large river. There were also several small villages to house
those farmers who did not dwell in the urban center. The urban
center, fields, canals, and villages together made up a city-state,
which functioned as an independent nation.

Drawbacks of Using the Rivers

**As McNeill points out, people who lived along the Tigris and
Euphrates rivers had to accept certain drawbacks along with
the benefits of using these waterways.**

In a year of low floods, the water might not suf-
fice to reach the more distant fields. Far more
dangerous were the years when the flood waters
rolled with unusual force, for then main dikes and
channels might be obliterated. And from time to
time the mighty Euphrates itself changed course,
leaving populated areas helpless against the com-
ing drought unless the irrigation works could be
remodeled in time. . . . By a cruel irony . . . populations dependent on dikes and canals exposed
themselves to periodic disaster.

Rivalries and Wars

Fierce independence among the Sumerian cities instigated rivalries. Disagreements over land, water use, and other issues often led to battles and wars between neighboring city-states. Each state, wrote Samuel N. Kramer, a professor and leading scholar on Sumerian history and language, was "eager to control as much as possible of the rich, irrigated land in and about its borders, [so] strife and contention became ever more frequent and violent. . . . What had started as limited economic rivalries turned into bitter political struggles for power, prestige, and territory."

At first, these wars fought near the banks of the twin rivers were small-scale. Usually, one city fought a single neighbor until the ongoing dispute was settled, either through military defeat or negotiation. Even with this fighting, the urban centers usually emerged intact thanks to their high protective walls.

Eventually, however, political and military strategy changed, and leaders of city-states began waging long, large-scale wars of conquest and imperialism

Wall painting in a late Assyrian house in Assur, from the time of Sargon II, who ruled from 721 to 705 BC. Sargon (left) is shown paying homage to the god Assur, the chief god of the Assyrian pantheon.

in order to increase their riches and expand their domains. In the 2300s BC, a Mesopotamian named Sargon conquered most of the region's city-states and established the world's first empire.

For the most part, the achievements of the local river civilization were positive. Networks of canals gave farmers greater access to water for their crops. These waterways also increased commerce between neighboring communities. Large-scale agriculture in the river valleys gave people access to a constant, abundant supply of food. As a result, the population and territory of these communities increased, and villages and towns became bustling cities and city-states. Thanks to the development of writing systems, these larger settlements could be organized according to written laws. The breakthrough of written language also made it possible for people to document their stories, creating a literary culture.

These developments generally improved living and working conditions in Mesopotamia. But the transition from small-scale villages to large-scale cities—and eventually empires—also made life more complex. As communities, cities, and nations grew larger and more advanced, they struggled to maintain their identity, independence, and influence in the region. Rivalries ensued, and these often led to war, which threatened not only the people but also the very land around the rivers that had given the people life.

Chapter Two:
Life in the First Cities

Sumerian domination of Mesopotamia ended around 2000 BC. In the centuries that followed, other peoples vied for control of the vast Tigris-Euphrates valley, which stretched from Syria and Palestine in the west to the Persian Gulf in the east. Chief among them were the Babylonians and Assyrians. The Babylonian cities were mainly in the south and east, in the former region of Sumer. The Assyrian cities were situated mostly in the hillier, somewhat drier north and west.

One major facet of this river civilization (as well as other major river civilizations) was continuity. People venerated tradition. They took pride in the customs, beliefs, and achievements of their ancestors. Social and other forms of change occurred very slowly. And for long periods, dress styles, religious ideas, and the layout and architectural styles of cities remained largely the same from one generation to the next. Everyday life in the cities along the rivers was little different in Babylonian times than it had been when Sumerians ran these cities. Even later, after the 500s BC, when Iranians, Greeks, and other outsiders took over the Mesopotamian plains, the pace of change remained very slow. As a result, life in and around the cities did not change very much. "While the physical image of the Mesopotamian city underwent changes and improvements over the centuries, many of its less tangible aspects were impervious to time," according to Samuel Kramer. "Social, political, religious, and economic patterns that arose in the world's first urban communities, those of the Sumerians, largely characterized all later Mesopotamian cities."

Layout of Cities and Houses

The theme of continuity in Mesopotamia is no better illustrated than in the layout of its cities and construction of its houses. Even today, there are sections of Iraqi towns and some urban and rural houses that closely resemble those of the region's first cities. Many of those cities were closely connected to and dependent on the nearby river or the major canals flowing from that waterway. Yale University scholar Karen R. Nemet-Nejat describes the general look of a Mesopotamian city as "crowded with houses, workshops, shrines, and other structures." She adds:

> Excavations of the city of Mashkan-shapir have provided the best picture of the layout of a southern Mesopotamian city to date. . . . [The main roads] ran either parallel to canals or at right angles to them, with bridges or ferries to link neighborhoods. The residential areas were connected by a network of streets, and most homes were entered through narrow alleyways and culs-de-sac [dead ends]. The layout of the narrow streets was like a maze. The street surfaces were uneven, in part due to the constant rebuilding of homes on previous foundations that were never leveled, and in part because garbage was

dumped into the streets. Dogs and other scaveng-
ing animals ate some rubbish, but the rest was
dried by the sun and walked on.

The houses in and around the Mesopotamian cities were of
a few basic and long-enduring types. Foundations and other
remnants of these dwellings have been discovered, and find-
ings indicate that most were made of mud, or clay, bricks. In
order to make such bricks, one shaped the moist clay (often
reinforced with straw) in a rectangular wooden mold, then
left the clay out in the sun to dry. (These bricks could also be
baked in kilns, which made them harder and more permanent.
But this method was also more expensive and used only for
building wealthy homes and shrines.)

Builders Responsible for Their Work

In some Mesopotamian cities and empires, local laws required
builders to use certain accepted construction materials
and methods. Those who did shoddy work were often sub-
ject to legal penalties. This is shown in some Babylonian
regulations:

"If a builder build a house for some one, even though he has
not yet completed it, [and] if then the walls seem [to be] top-
pling, the builder must make the walls solid from his own
means [i.e., at his own expense]."

"If a builder build a house for some one, and does not construct
it properly, and the house which he built fall in and kill its
owner, then that builder shall be put to death."

Most of the mud-brick houses, both inside and outside the cities, were small because poor people lived in them. Typically, they had a single main room and sometimes one or two smaller rooms adjoining it. Wealthy families, which made up a small fraction of the population, could afford larger homes. The houses of successful merchants, government officials, and big landowners had seven, eight, or more rooms. According to Stephen Bertman, of the University of Windsor:

> A comfortable home made of brick would feature a central roofed courtyard around which smaller rooms would be grouped. In ancient Babylon, such a courtyard might have measured something like 8 by 18 feet. . . . [The] kitchen could be a separate room, but often it was incorporated into the courtyard with an open brick hearth built against a wall. . . . Other rooms, some of which would interconnect, would have included a living room, bedrooms . . . [and] servants' quarters.

Ancient city of Kharanaq

Most Mesopotamian houses had no bathrooms. The common custom was to relieve oneself into a small clay container. When the container was full, one dumped its contents into a pit dug in the ground. To bathe, people typically went to the nearby river or canal. Only well-to-do homes had bathrooms with toilets, many of which were equipped with buckets beneath the seats to catch wastes. Even fewer houses had drainage systems because they were expensive to build and maintain. In such a system, Bertman says, "A tiled drain in the lowest part of the floor would carry away waste and wastewater to a cesspool, or, if a primitive sewer system existed in a city, all the way to the river."

Another common kind of home was found in the villages of Mesopotamia's countryside, especially in the marshy areas near the rivers and canals. Such a house, which usually had only one room, was fashioned from bundles of river reeds. The peasants who lived in these humble dwellings also used reeds to make canoes for catching fish and baskets for storing food and other items.

Furniture and Food

In fact, reed baskets, or chests constructed of baked clay or palm wood, were used for storage in all Mesopotamian homes, rich or poor. Closets were not yet used. Other common furnishings included stools and chairs made of wood or woven reeds; low wooden tables used for eating meals; and beds made of reed mats or mattresses stuffed with palm fibers. Richer folk were able to afford softer mattresses stuffed with wool or goat's hair. They could also afford the luxury of woolen blankets.

The meals served and eaten on the wooden tables varied according to what the family could afford. The average Mesopotamian, who was poor, or nearly so, ate mainly bread and porridge made from barley, wheat, or other grains. He or she also enjoyed a few vegetables and fruits. These included

A young woman weaving a reed basket

garlic, onions, peas, cabbage, lentils, carrots, dates, figs, and plums. People ate fish if they or someone they knew could catch them in the river. However, poor people usually could not afford to eat meat.

In contrast, members of the upper classes typically ate meat almost every day. The most common kinds of meat in the region were pork, mutton (from sheep), deer, and gazelle (along with geese and other birds). The well-to-do also had full-time cooks, as well as servants to assist the cooks, bring the food to the table, and clean up afterward.

Whether one prepared one's own food or had a cook and servants to do so, kitchens were basically the same. As Nemet-Nejat explains:

> Food was prepared in an oven, found within the house or in the courtyard. Pots were made with small handles through which a rope could be passed to hang them out of the reach of rats and mice. Other cooking utensils included a copper frying pan, a sieve pot, and kettles for water. . . . Smaller jars were used for [cooking] oil, clarified butter, or beer. A mortar and pestle, made of baked clay or stone, were used to pound some cereal foods . . . [and] hand mills, made from imported volcanic rock, were used for grinding barley, sesame seeds, and spices.

Mortar and pestle

An Ancient Recipe

This surviving ancient Mesopotamian recipe dates from about 1700 BC. It is for a dish called "braised turnips."

Meat is not needed. [First] boil [some] wate Throw fat in. [Add] onion, dorsal thorn [name of unknown plant used as seasoning], coriander, cumin and kanašû [a legume]. Squeeze leek and garlic and spread [juice] on dish. Add onion and mint.

Marriage and Divorce

Cooking was almost always women's work—so were cleaning and looking after the children. This was partly because of the long-standing tradition that the husband (or father, or other chief male) was the head of the family. Such a social arrangement is said to be patriarchal, or male-dominated. Because she was legally and socially inferior, the wife (or mother) had to follow her husband's rules. And any daughters they produced had to remain obedient to their father until they got married. After that they had to do the bidding of their own husbands.

Love—the romantic kind seen in modern movies—did exist in Mesopotamia, but it was rarely a factor in choosing a mate. The vast majority of marriages were arranged by relatives (usually fathers or grandfathers). The marital union was seen mainly as a business arrangement, and the parties involved drew up a legal contract. As part of the deal, the bride's father supplied a dowry, consisting of items of value, such as jewelry, furniture, slaves, or bars of silver. The husband was to use these things for his wife's upkeep in the marriage.

As often happens today, Mesopotamian marriages did not always work out. Some unhappy couples chose to divorce. A wife could seek a divorce if her husband beat or otherwise abused her, but she had to prove the mistreatment. One of the laws created by Hammurabi, the eighteenth-century BC Babylonian king, stated:

> If a woman quarrels with her husband, and say: "You are not congenial to me [i.e., mistreat me]," the reasons for her prejudice must be presented. [If] there is no fault on her part, but he leaves and neglects her, then no guilt attaches to this woman, she shall take her dowry and go back to her father's house.

Making Money

The strong emphasis that Mesopotamians placed on dowries and upkeep of wives and families in marriage demonstrates the importance of money and work in their society. Most people were poor. They did their best to make ends meet as farmers, laborers, or craftsmen. Among the far fewer prosperous people were landowners and successful merchants. The latter made their livings by exploiting lucrative trade routes that ran through the region.

For this river civilization, "trade was of a very great importance from the earliest time," as noted scholar on Mesopotamia and professor at London's University of the Arts Gwendolyn Leick points out. "Because communication within cities in the [river valley] was generally by waterways and on boats, the commercial district which concerned itself with inter-city and long-distance trade was located near the landing quays and known as karum: 'harbor'. . . . As an institution it had an important function for the city, since it allowed the movement of goods produced locally . . . and the receipt of raw materials [from foreign regions]."

These imported goods, along with ones produced locally, were regularly on sale in large outdoor markets similar to those seen in the Middle East today. For many centuries coins and

Goods available at an Iranian open market today

paper money did not exist. People bought and sold items using the barter system, which consists of paying for something with an object of equal value to the item being purchased. To determine the value of an item, Mesopotamian officials utilized the existing value of silver. They used carefully calibrated scales to weigh sale items and to compare them to given weights of silver.

Honest vs. Dishonest Merchants

This passage from a surviving Babylonian hymn stresses that there were both honest and dishonest merchants, and that it ultimately paid to be honest.

The merchant who [practices] trickery as he holds the balances [scales], who uses two sets of weights [one real, the other phony] is disappointed in the matter of profit and [eventually] loses [his money]. The honest merchant who holds the balances [and gives] good weight, [eventually triumphs because] everything is presented to him in good measure.

Cinnamon sticks and other spices

Taking a Break

Whether one was a farmer, merchant, laborer, or craftsman, Mesopotamians, like people today, needed to take a break sometimes. The leisure activities available in those days were not as numerous and diverse as those today, but they were perfectly adequate for people who worked extremely long hours and had very little free time.

Gambling is a good example of a popular leisure activity. Men throughout the Tigris-Euphrates valley enjoyed playing games of chance, particularly dice games. The dice they used had four triangular-shaped surfaces. Before coins came into use (in the mid-first millennium BC), the players did not wager for actual money; instead, they bet objects of value, including weapons, sheep, goats, clothes, jewelry, and so forth.

Dice were also used in board games—like the one found by archaeologists in the ruins of the Sumerian city of Ur. The game board is made of wood and decorated by tiny pieces of red limestone and white shells. About the size of a computer keyboard, it has twenty-one squares. Each player had seven playing pieces, but how these were used, as well as the object of the game, remains a mystery.

More vigorous physical games were also popular in Mesopotamia. Wealthy individuals, including kings, enjoyed sport-hunting that involved horses, chariots, wagons, and traps, and required many helpers to find and manage the animals. One Assyrian king, Tiglathpileser I (reigned circa 1115–1077 BC), claimed to have bagged lions, tigers, bears, deer, hyenas, bison, wild pigs, gazelle, elephants, and ostriches.

Various Mesopotamian peoples, including the Sumerians, Babylonians, and Assyrians, also enjoyed competitive sports, such as horse-racing, archery, and wrestling, which is likely the world's oldest sport. The wrestlers wore belts around their hips. One common offensive move was to grab hold of the opponent's belt and pull him off balance. Some wrestling matches were described in literature—the most famous example is the *Epic of Gilgamesh*. In it, the title character engaged in a rough-and-tumble brawl similar to those staged in modern pro-wrestling matches.

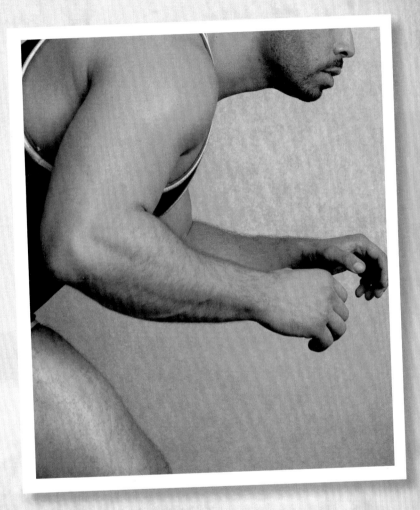

Modern wrestling evolved from ancient versions, including those practiced in Mesopotamia.

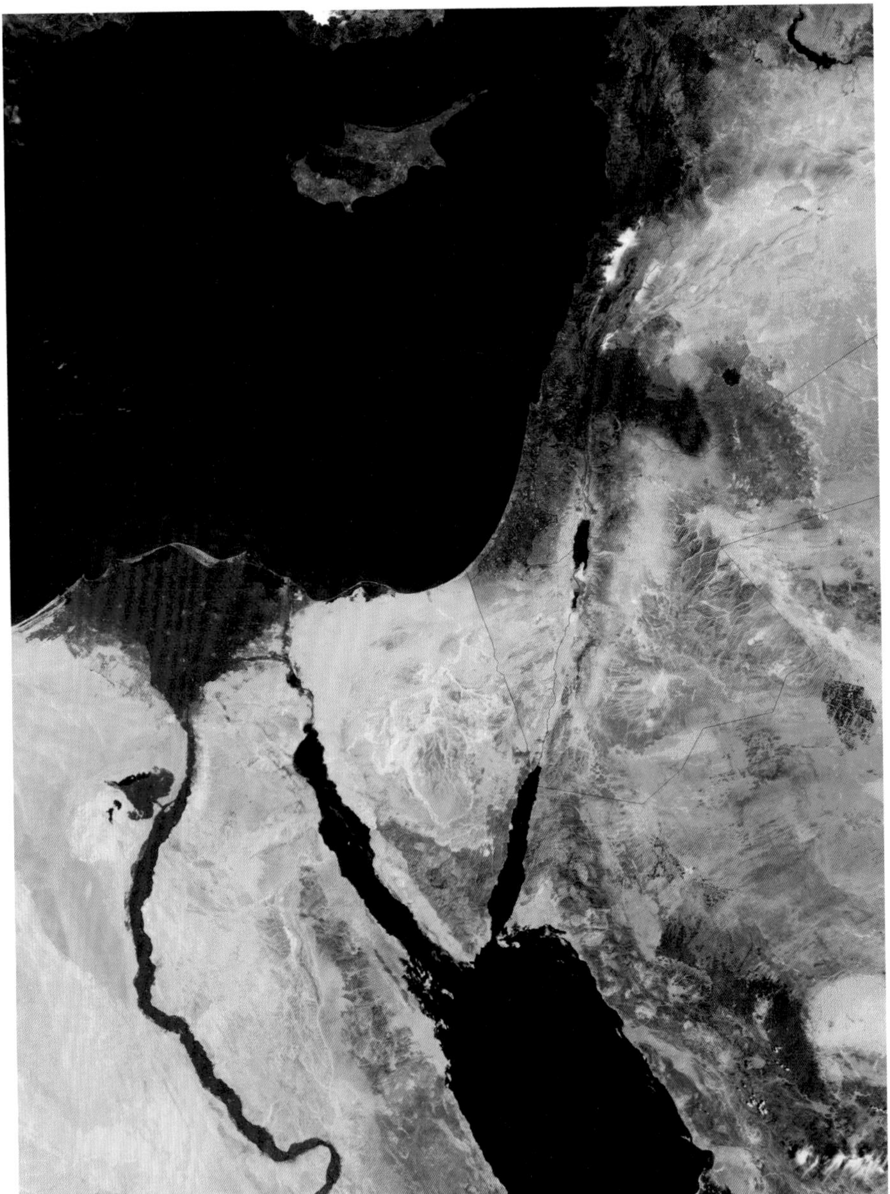

Satellite image of the Middle East. Visible in the image are the countries of Egypt, Israel, Jordan, Saudi Arabia, Syria, and the island of Cyprus. The major bodies of water are the Mediterranean Sea, the Red Sea, the Dead Sea, and the Nile River.

Chapter Three:
The Gift of the River

While Mesopotamia gave the world its first cities, Egypt gave it its first large nation-state. That nation arose in about 3100 BC, not long after Uruk and other Mesopotamian towns expanded into true cities. Like the cultures of the Tigris-Euphrates valley, Egyptian civilization grew up along the banks of a mighty river—the Nile. The world's longest river, it starts in the mountains of eastern Africa. It flows more than 4,130 miles northward, passing through Egypt and emptying into the Mediterranean Sea.

The livable sector of the Nile Valley was (and remains) quite narrow. The strip of fertile land capable of supporting large numbers of people measures only four to thirteen miles wide. The rest of Egypt is mostly arid and much of it is desert, which made the Nile absolutely essential to ancient Egyptian life. People used its waters for drinking, bathing, and watering crops. They also traveled on it, using boats, both up- and downstream. Because the river flows from south to north, the southern, downstream region became known as Upper Egypt; the northern, upstream portion was called Lower Egypt.

Rise of Egyptian Farming

Upper and Lower Egypt played crucial roles in Egyptian history and life both before and after the great turning point of 3100 BC. The first people who lived more or less permanently in the region were hunter-gatherers, like early Mesopotamian peoples. Evidence shows that they lived in caves or fragile shelters made of river reeds or tree branches. Apparently they sustained themselves mainly by following herds of game animals up and down the river banks

Sometime shortly after 6000 BC, immigrants from Palestine, in the Fertile Crescent, began entering Lower Egypt. They already practiced agriculture, which had begun in the Crescent a few thousand years before. And they introduced food-growing techniques to the Nile Valley. Over time, most of the area's inhabitants learned to grow a wide variety of crops. The most widely raised were wheat and barley, says Fekri Hassan, professor emeritus at University College London. Egyptians used these grains to make "bread, cakes and a nutritious type of beer. [These were] supplemented by fava beans, lentils, and peas . . . lettuces, cucumbers, leeks, onions and radishes. Among the most popular fruits [were] melons, dates, sycamore figs and pomegranates. Grapes were also cultivated and were used to make both red and white wines. . . . Farmers also kept sheep, goats, cattle and pigs."

The next important turning point in the long saga of Egyptian civilization occurred sometime in the 4000s BC. For the first time on a large scale, Egyptian farmers incorporated the Nile's yearly, mostly gentle floods into their food production process. These floods were called the inundation. As University of Manchester professor Rosalie David explains:

> The rains fall every year on the highlands [of] tropical Africa and increase the waters of the Nile so that . . . the river became swollen and flooded out over its banks, depositing the rich

black silt that fertilized the land. In Egypt the flood occurred first in [Upper Egypt] in late June. The effect reached [Lower Egypt] at the end of September, and then the waters gradually receded until they reached their lowest level in the following April. This annual miracle brought renewed life to the parched land and was eagerly awaited by all inhabitants of the country.

Taking advantage of the inundation enabled the Egyptians to grow far more food than before, and this increase in production stimulated a steady growth in population. Villages sprang up throughout the Nile Valley. In this way, the river made the beginnings of a great nation possible, as the Greek historian Herodotus observed when he visited Egypt in the 400s BC. He called Egyptian civilization "the gift of the river."

Reverence for the River

The Egyptians were so thankful for what the Nile and its yearly floods gave them that they revered a divine spirit, Hapy, god of the inundation. During worship, they sang a hymn to Hapy, with lyrics that read in part:

He waters the landscape the sun god has formed, giving life to every small creature. . . . Loved by the waiting earth, he nurtures the new-born grain. . . . Food bringer, rich with provisions, himself the author of all his good things, awe-striking master, yet sweet the aromas arising about him, and how he satisfies when he returns!—transforming the dust to pastures for cattle . . . filling the storerooms, heaping the grainsheds, giving his gifts to the poor.

From Villages to a Nation

As the fourth millennium (3000s) BC dawned, both Egypt and its sister civilization, Mesopotamia, had several similarities. Each was dependent on a major river (in the case of Mesopotamia, two rivers). Each practiced large-scale agriculture and used river water to irrigate its crops. And the residents of each dwelled in villages and small towns.

Later in that millennium, however, the two civilizations diverged in a major way. Some of Mesopotamia's towns began growing into cities, which soon became independent city-states. In contrast, Egypt's towns stayed towns, but started to come together to form larger and larger political units.

The first of these units were the nomes. (*Nome* was the later Greek word for such a unit. The Egyptian word for it was *sepat*.) Each nome was a small province consisting of several neighboring villages and their surrounding farmlands. Eventually there were forty-two nomes, twenty in Lower Egypt and twenty-two in Upper Egypt.

Sometime around 3400 BC (give or take a century) each group of nomes formed a larger political unit—a kingdom. What made it a kingdom was that it had a king who ruled over all of its nomes and villages. The northern kingdom, which included the fertile Nile Delta, became known as the Red Land; the southern kingdom came to be called the White Land. Very little is known about these realms and their rulers, largely because they had no known written records.

Although historians have very little information about these kingdoms, they suspect that the two kingdoms developed an energetic rivalry. Disputes over territory and trade likely incited battles and wars between the two lands. One piece of surviving evidence for such conflicts is a series of carved figures on the head of a limestone war club. Supposedly this club was the property of a king of the White Land, and a number of the figures appear to be war captives. If that is the case, the ruler in question may have attacked the Red Land and managed to take some prisoners.

It was another king of the White Land who accomplished the final and biggest step in Egypt's political unification process. His name was Narmer. (Various ancient sources also call him Menes, Meni, or Min.) In about 3100 BC, he brought together Upper and Lower Egypt and established the world's first major nation-state.

The Narmer Palette

One way that Narmer celebrated his unification of the two kingdoms was by commissioning works of art. These pieces were both attractive and an effective means of propaganda. One of them has come to be called the "Narmer Palette." A flat stone carved on both sides, it is about twenty-five inches long. Scholar and museum curator Rita Freed describes it:

> The main image on the palette is dominated by a large-scale representation of King Narmer himself. . . . His head is rendered in true profile, but the eye is represented frontally, in part because this effect was easier to achieve successfully, but also because the eye was considered the most important element of the face. The broad shoulders are also shown frontally to emphasize the king's strength and power.

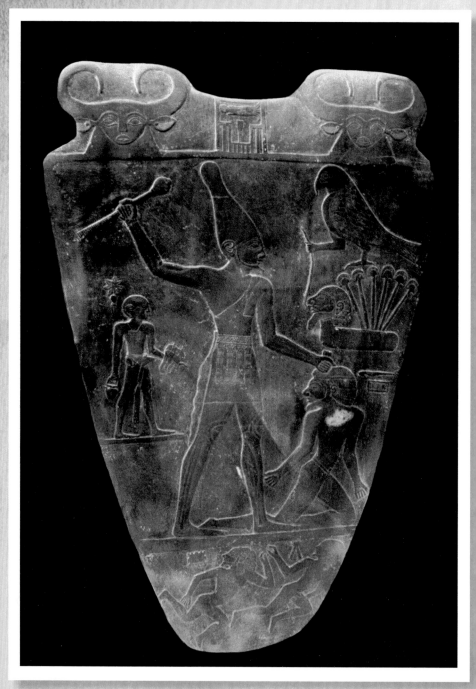

The Narmer Palette. It shows the first pharaoh, Narmer, of Egypt in battle to unite his country.

Egypt's First Dynasty and the God-King

Because he was the first king, or pharaoh, of a united Egypt, Narmer established the nation's first dynasty, or family line of rulers. Eight more rulers followed him in that dynasty, and ancient Egypt was destined to have more than thirty more dynasties in its long history.

Narmer also founded a new capital city for the unified country not far south of the Nile Delta. It was called Memphis, then meaning "White Fortress." The central government was located in the capital. Although the pharaoh was the head of that government, he could not run it all by himself. He appointed a chief administrator, called a vizier, to oversee the various government departments.

In addition to introducing new institutions, Narmer wisely bowed to tradition and kept several older ones in place. The nomes remained, for example, and so did the tradition of the two ancient kingdoms. Narmer and all of his successors called themselves kings of the "Two Lands." To emphasize this symbolism, they wore a crown that merged elements of the crowns of the kings of the Red and White lands.

The First Dynasty was also significant because it firmly established the concept of the God-King. The pharaohs came to be seen not only as all-powerful rulers, but also as semi-divine beings. It was believed that the pharaoh had to be in contact with the gods in order for the nation to remain in a state of order and harmony. This state, constituting the opposite of chaos, was called ma'at.

Egyptians' belief in the principle of ma'at and view of their king as godlike was part of a larger phenomenon: their extreme and sincere piety, based on their devotion to the traditional gods. "Religion permeated an Egyptian's total existence," wrote renowned classics professor Lionel Casson. "In his eyes, every detail of his own life, and of the life about him [was] a specific, calculated act of a god."

"The Pharaoh was a God"

The religiously devout Egyptians believed that everything that happened in nature was the work of one or more gods. In the words of Casson:

> We of the West can place religion in a compartment all its own, we can say, "Render unto Caesar the things that are Caesar's and to God the things that are God's," but not an Egyptian. His Caesar was the pharaoh, and the pharaoh was a god. . . . The monuments of Egyptian architecture are all religious—pyramids and other types of tombs, temple chapels [and] sanctums. . . . Even in politics the [all-encompassing] presence of religion is clear. The great administrative officials at the pharaoh's court were at the same time [priests] of the church.

Common Religious Rituals

In fact, of all the major ancient river civilizations, Egypt's was arguably the most concerned with and consumed by religious beliefs and worship. These ideas and rituals were not based on a particular creed or sacred writing. (For example, Christians have the Bible, Jews the Torah, and Muslims the Koran.) Rather, the Egyptian religion was based on actions performed by the faithful to honor or communicate with the gods. These actions included offering sacrifices (gifts) to the gods; prayer; taking part in public festivals that honored the gods; and tending to the upkeep of the gods' statues and temples. Egyptians believed that maintaining these rituals would ensure their favorable standing with the gods and safeguard the earth against the gods' wrath. In contrast, if people neglected these rituals, the gods might destroy the world and people along with it.

The rituals of prayer and sacrifice could and did take place almost anywhere, though people most often performed them in their homes. The most common form of sacrifice involved slaughtering an animal and burning certain parts of it. Like other ancient peoples, the Egyptians thought that the smoke from such a sacred fire ascended into the sky and satisfied the gods. After the sacrifice, as part of the ritual, the worshipers cooked and ate the rest of the animal.

As for prayers, Egyptians usually began with words that followed set formulas. One often-repeated formula was: "Hail to you Ra, Lord of Truth." The worshiper would then heap praises on the god and finally make some kind of request. Common requests were for recovery from sickness, plentiful harvests, and victory in battle.

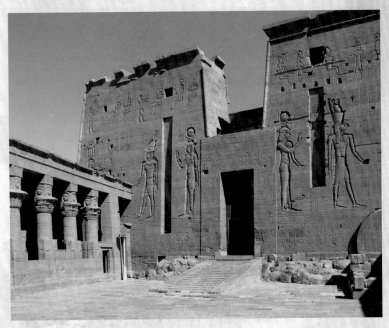

Ancient temple of Isis, Egyptian goddess of fertility

Ram-headed sphinx, symbol of the Egyptian god Amun-Ra, standing over a statue of the Pharaoh Ramesses II at the Karnak Temple in Luxor, Egypt

One place where ordinary people did not conduct worship was inside the religious temples, as people do in churches, synagogues, and mosques today. Only priests and their various assistants and servants could enter an Egyptian temple. The priests were not spiritual guides for congregations of worshipers, as modern priests and ministers are. Instead, as one noted modern scholar explains:

> [A priest] was employed at the temple to look after the cult statue of the deity. Like mortals, the god or goddess was thought to have daily needs for food and clothing. Most priests would not have come into contact with the cult image, and, in theory, only the pharaoh, the high priest of every cult, had the privilege of attending the god. In practice, however, his authority was delegated to the chief priest, who was supported by lesser priests, who would have attended to offerings and minor parts of the temple ritual.

Although their jobs within a temple varied, all Egyptian priests followed certain strict rules in their daily lives. Herodotus listed some of these rules:

> The priests shave their bodies all over every other day to guard against the presence of lice, or anything else equally unpleasant, while they are about their religious duties. The priests, too, wear linen only, and shoes made from the papyrus plant—these materials, for dress and shoes, being the only ones allowed them. They bath in cold water twice a day and twice every night—and observe innumerable other [rules and] ceremonies besides.

Egyptian priests carrying an offering

Combining Devotion and Enjoyment

Both priests and ordinary worshipers did come together a few times each year in traditional religious festivals. One of the oldest celebrations—the New Year Festival—was connected directly to the Nile River. It took place on July 19, the official beginning of the river's yearly inundation. This event was considered so important that it was also reckoned as the first day of the year on the national calendar.

Another and even more spectacular celebration was the Festival of Opet. It gained its greatest level of importance in the second millennium BC. The festival occurred in the midst of the flood season and lasted from two to four weeks. A huge and splendid procession (solemn parade) was staged along one bank of the Nile. Priests, followed by thousands of worshipers, marched along carrying sacred images of three gods: the supreme god, Amun-Ra; his close follower, Mut; and his son, Khonsu. The priests took the statues of these deities from one temple and bore them down a wide road lined by stone sphinxes to a second temple.

After the procession, the celebration continued. People sacrificed, prayed, sang and danced, held large feasts, and in general had a good time. In this way, they combined religious praise with the enjoyment of social activities.

The Egyptians demonstrated their faith through other large-scale, national activities, too. For example, they joined together by the thousands to build gigantic tombs for the kings they revered. The result of these grand efforts is evident even today, many thousands of years later, for these immense monuments—the great pyramids—still stand and remain among the wonders of the world.

Chapter Four:
Builders of the Pyramids

All of the major ancient river civilizations left behind imposing physical monuments as testimonials to their greatness. In China it was the famous Great Wall, which stretched for some 4,000 miles. In Mesopotamia, it was cities, each covering several square miles, and ziggurats, massive structures that supported temples.

But none have captured the imaginations of successive generations over the course of millennia as much as the great pyramids at Giza, in northern Egypt. They have become in a real sense that country's trademark, as well as objects of awe and mystery. People still argue over how they were built and marvel at the dark passages and tombs hidden inside them.

Scholars and avid buffs of ancient Egyptian culture see them as markers of a great transition in mankind's long and eventful story. Like Mesopotamia's cities, the great pyramids symbolize the victory of agriculture over hunting and gathering. That major turning point spawned permanent settlements, especially in the great river valleys, and made possible the march of civilization to the present. "The pyramids are . . .

The Great Pyramids at Giza

more than mere wonders," wrote Desmond Stewart, a British journalist who authored many books about Egypt. "They are triumphal monuments to a momentous revolution in human history: the decisive changeover from the five thousand centuries in which men were nomads to our relatively brief experience of growing food in settled communities."

From Mastabas to Pyramids

The ancient Egyptians themselves did not think of the pyramids in this same way. They did view them as monuments, to be sure, but not as tributes to the agricultural revolution. Instead they were monuments to individuals—impressive and often grand tombs for kings, queens, and a few other high-status people.

In all, more than ninety pyramid-tombs of various sizes were erected in ancient Egypt. Most of these great edifices appeared in the period that modern historians call the Old Kingdom, lasting from 2686 to 2181 BC, or about five centuries. For that reason, the Old Kingdom is often informally called the "pyramid age." The largest and most famous pyramids were built in an even shorter interval, the Fourth Dynasty (2613–2494 BC). It is these relatively few giant structures that people think of when they hear the words "pyramids of Egypt." And appropriately, the pharaohs of that dynasty are frequently referred to as the "pyramid-builders."

Other than their enormous size, there was little that was new about tombs of the Fourth-Dynasty kings. Smaller pyramids had been built during the Third Dynasty (2686–2613 BC). These were part of an evolution of impressive royal tombs that had begun before Narmer unified the Red and White lands circa 3100 BC.

In that earlier age, called the Predynastic Period, kings and other nobles were buried in structures known as mastabas. Each mastaba had an above-ground section, or superstructure, and a below-ground section, the substructure. According to Rosalie David:

> The superstructure was rectangular and bench-shaped, hence the term used by Egyptologists: Mastaba is the Arabic word for "bench-shaped." In earliest times (from c.3400 BC) it was built entirely of mud brick. [Later] there was increasing use of stone. . . . The superstructure marked the location of the tomb and protected the burial and also provided a place where food offerings [to the deceased] could be brought. . . . [Meanwhile] the substructure housed the burial chamber and was the equivalent of the domestic bedroom. There was also sometimes a second chamber to accommodate the burial of the owner's wife, and there were storage areas for goods and possessions.

The oldest standing step pyramid in Egypt, designed by Imhotep for King Djoser. It is located in Saqqara, an ancient burial ground about nineteen miles south of modern-day Cairo.

These goods and possessions, including food, clothes, and weapons, were essential to the burial. The Egyptians believed that the deceased would need these items to survive in the afterlife.

One reason the builders eventually switched to using stone rather than mud bricks for such tombs was durability. Mud bricks disintegrated fairly quickly, making it easier for tomb-robbers to break into and loot the burial chambers. Using stone made it harder for the thieves to get in; it also made the tombs last longer.

Another way to increase the strength and durability of mastabas was to make them larger. A talented and bright architect and builder of the Third Dynasty, Imhotep, used larger mastabas in his projects and introduced a major innovation in architecture and engineering. He was charged with building the tomb of that dynasty's second ruler, Djoser (or Zoser), who reigned from 2667 to 2648 BC. At first Imhotep was planning to construct the biggest mastaba Egypt had ever seen. Work began on the monument at Saqqara, a few miles north of the capital, Memphis. But at some point the architect decided to combine several mastabas into a single, much larger structure. He built a slightly smaller mastaba atop the initial one. Then he added four more successively smaller mastabas above the second one, for a total of six. The resulting structure was the first pyramid-tomb, which soared to a height of almost two hundred feet. Because the edges of the mastabas formed indentations, or steps, along the sides, it became known as the Step Pyramid of Saqqara.

Other pharaohs of the Third Dynasty commissioned step pyramids to be erected. Among them were Sekhemkhet, who followed Djoser on the throne, and Khaba, who succeeded Seckhemkhet. It was the architects of the first pharaoh of the Fourth Dynasty, Sneferu, who introduced the idea of filling in the steps on the sides of a pyramid. By doing this, they transformed a step pyramid at Meidum, south of Memphis, into the first smooth-sided, or true, pyramid. After that, true pyramids became the rule in Egypt.

A Stairway to Heaven

There were two major reasons the pyramidal shape became so popular for royal tombs in ancient Egypt, and both were rooted in religion. First, the Egyptians believed that the original, sacred mound of creation, the benben, had been pyramid-shaped. Second, they held that after his death, the pharaoh whose body lay inside the pyramid would use the side of the structure as an initial stairway in his journey to heaven. The following words were found in a very old group of Egyptian writings known as the Pyramid Texts: "He [the pharaoh] rusheth at the sky as a heron; he hath kissed the sky as a hawk. . . . [And] he ascendeth into the sky among his brethren, the gods. . . . A ramp to the sky is built for him that he may go up to the sky."

Khufu's Horizon

Sneferu erected three more large pyramids, all of which began construction as smooth-sided pyramids. These structures, along with later royal pyramids, also had other features that made them stand out. First, each was surrounded by a number of other buildings, altogether forming a pyramid complex. There were traditional mastabas, and sometimes smaller pyramids, in which the pharaoh's family members were interred. There was also a mortuary temple. It had a staff of priests whose job was to perform rituals that helped the deceased king prosper in the afterlife.

"The mortuary temple," writes Desmond Stewart, "was the focus of the cult of the dead king once he was entombed inside his pyramid. Here the priests would daily deposit a meal in the innermost shrine. Only the essence of the food would be tasted by the [pharaoh's spirit]. The untouched remains would be removed the following morning and replaced."

In addition, a pyramid complex usually had stone causeways (sometimes lined with sphinxes or other statues), one or more chapels, and a sturdy protective outer wall. Particularly large and lavish complexes of this sort were constructed around the largest pyramids of all. These were the tombs of Sneferu's son, Khufu (reigned 2589–2566 BC), and grandson, Khafre (2558–2532 BC). (These were their Egyptian names. Some modern books still refer to them by their later Greek names, Cheops and Chephren.) They were erected at Giza, on the Nile's west bank a few miles southwest of modern-day Cairo.

Khufu's pyramid was and remains the largest of all the giant tombs built in ancient Egypt. He, his builders, and his followers called the amazing structure Akhet-Khufu, meaning "Khufu's Horizon." When first built, it was 481 feet (147m) high and 756 feet (230m) on each side of its immense base. (Today, the monument is about thirty feet shorter. This is primarily because the white limestone blocks that originally formed its

The blocks of stone used to make the Great Pyramids

outer casing were torn away in medieval times to be used in the construction of buildings in nearby Cairo.)

Modern visitors to Giza often remark that Khafre's pyramid, the smaller of the two giants, looks a little larger than Khufu's. There are two reasons for this. First, Khafre's tomb was erected on a slightly higher level of the local plateau. Also, some of the original casing stones remain atop Khafre's pyramid. So it still maintains a height of 478 feet (146m). A third and considerably smaller pyramid on the plateau is that of Khafre's successor, Menkaura. It is about 220 feet (67m) tall, making it slightly bigger than Djoser's pyramid at Saqqara.

The Harbor at Giza

The Nile River played an important role in the building and maintenance of the great pyramids at Giza, as explained by Jill Kamil, a noted historian and journalist who lives in Egypt:

> The core of Khufu's pyramid was built of local limestone, which was mined from the main quarry on the plateau. . . . [But] the facing stone from Tura [on the river's east bank] had to be transported . . . across the river. During the annual inundation, the high level of the Nile would have enabled ships to approach the Giza plateau. The idea of a harbor at Giza, long suspected, has now been confirmed with the discovery of what appears to be the ruins of a stone pier. Perhaps it was fed by a canal during low Nile, so that shallow-bottomed vessels with their heavy loads could moor there all year round. It is likely that there was also a network of smaller canals dug off the main waterway to transport food for the workers.

Workers and Methods

These gigantic structures were built essentially by stacking enormous numbers of large, heavy stone blocks on top of one another. Modern sources estimate that Khufu's pyramid alone required more than 2.3 million separate blocks. Each weighed an average of two and a half tons. Making this feat even more impressive was the fact that construction tools and methods in Old-Kingdom Egypt were quite basic. Even the rudimentary block-and-tackle (a combination of pulleys and ropes used for lifting) was unknown. Erecting these and other such large structures was accomplished mainly using simple levers and the raw muscle power of thousands of workers.

For a long time it was thought that the majority of these workers were slaves. This notion was based on later ancient writings, including Herodotus's book. He claimed that Khufu was a cruel ruler who "brought the country into all sorts of misery." Supposedly, the pharaoh forced his people "without exception to labor as slaves for his own advantage."

However, Herodotus lived more than two thousand years after Khufu did. And by that time the Egyptians themselves had largely forgotten how the pyramids had been built. Modern historians argue that the workers who raised these great monuments were not slaves. They were free Egyptians, mostly farmers. They labored on large public construction projects during periods when there was little or no planting or harvesting to be done. In the process, they also may have fulfilled certain tax obligations.

Some of the workers quarried the blocks of stone and brought them to the building site. Others dressed the stones. This involved trimming them with copper chisels and smoothing their surfaces by grinding them with pieces of sandstone. Meanwhile, gangs of workers made sure the base, or foundation, of the structure was level. Then they started stacking the stones in layers, or courses, a task that became increasingly difficult as the courses got higher. To reach the upper level, the workers piled up huge mounds of sand and dirt, forming earthen ramps around the unfinished building. Then they dragged the blocks up these ramps. When they were finished, they removed the sand and dirt.

His Aching Back

Among those who raised the pyramids were masons, or stone-cutters. A Twelfth Dynasty Egyptian document titled "Satire on the Trades" both captures and bemoans how hard they worked:

> The mason cutting with his chisel in all sort of hard and costly stone—after he finishes two cubic feet of work, his arms are dead and he himself is weary. He sits there until suppertime, knees cramped and with an aching back.

Masons dressed and laid limestone blocks to build the pyramids.

Where Did They Live?

Various modern estimates indicate that it took from 5,000 to more than 20,000 workers to carry out all of the required steps for building a pyramid. Because these laborers often worked away from home, they had to take up temporary residence somewhere near the construction sites. Throughout most of the twentieth century, the location of their quarters remained a mystery.

Scientists began solving this mystery in the 1990s. Egypt's chief archaeologist, Zahi Hawass, teamed up with American archaeologist Mark Lehner. Digging at a site on the Giza plateau not far from the great pyramids and the Nile's banks, they found the remains of a large workers' village. Hawass later wrote:

> We found a large Old Kingdom settlement about 3 km [1.8 miles] square. We recorded a continuous layer of mud-brick buildings starting about 165 feet south of the valley Temple of Khufu and extending about 1 mile to the south. Among the artifacts [excavated] are thousands of fragments of every day pottery and bread molds, cooking pots, beer jars and trays for sifting grain and flour . . . [as well as] domesticated animal bones, such as beef, pork and sheep with butchers' marks on them.

Nearby, Hawass and Lehner also discovered a cemetery containing the tombs of the workers. Compared to the pharaohs' imposing resting places, those of the lowly laborers were tiny and modest. The average grave of this sort was a hole dug in the sand and lined with some mud bricks. The deceased's family members covered the hole with a small stone grave marker.

A broad view of the Great Pyramids

What the excavators discovered inside these graves was even more illuminating than the tombs themselves. In addition to human remains, there were grave goods that grieving relatives had placed inside. These goods reveal a great deal about the workers and their lives. There were small statues of workers' family members, for instance.

"One of the statuettes," according to Hawass, "depicts a woman seated on a backless chair with her hands on her knees. An inscription on the chair identifies her as Hepeny-kawes. She wears a black wig with hair parted in the middle and reaching to her shoulders. . . . A second statuette, badly damaged by salt, depicts her husband, Kaihep. A third statuette is of a kneeling woman, possibly a servant, grinding grain."

These humble folk thought they were building monuments that would last forever. And in a sense they were right—nearly five millennia later, the Giza pyramids still stand as testaments to a once mighty civilization that owed nearly its entire life to the river.

Chapter Five:
A Blessing and a Curse

At roughly the same time that the Egyptians were erecting giant pyramids, the Sumerian cities were warring among themselves on the plains of Mesopotamia. During that same period—the mid-2000s BC—far to the east, another magnificent river civilization was beginning to take shape along the Yellow River, in northeastern China. There were no cities or kingdoms yet, but there were small agricultural villages similar to the ones that had existed in Mesopotamia and Egypt a thousand years before.

The Chinese appear to have developed agriculture at least by 5000 BC, and most scholars suspect that it happened several centuries earlier. Farmers along the Yellow River learned to grow millet and wheat; these crops thrived in the region's cool, semi-arid climate. Along the Yangtze River, further south, where the climate is warmer and wetter, people began growing rice. Yet it took several millennia for farming to become large-scale and for the first nation-states, or small kingdoms, to develop along the Yellow River. (The Yangtze farmers continued to grow food, but their region did not become politically

The Yellow River, in China

or culturally important until many centuries after civilization developed along the Yellow.)

The principal reason it took a long time for the Yellow River civilization to emerge may have been the unusual nature of that river. It flows from the high Tibetan plateau, through Mongolia, and into the immense North China Plain. The latter, the largest river plain in eastern Asia, covers some 158,000 square miles (410,000 sq. km). As it flows through, the river deposits layers of a very rich, yellowish-brown soil, called loess, onto the plain. On the one hand, this fertile soil made agriculture and civilization possible in China. On the other, it made the region, like the river, extremely difficult to tame and control. David C. Wright, of the University of Calgary, explains:

The Yellow River is both a blessing and a curse to China. Its greatest benefit is, of course, the water and fertile soil it carries. At the same time, the very loess that makes agriculture possible also creates its own hazards. It is so abundant and heavy that the river is constantly depositing. Over thousands of years the Yellow River has created its own beds and channels on the accumulated loess, and these are often higher than the surrounding countryside. The loess banks on the edges of the river form natural dikes that hold the river in its course. These dikes, however, are weak and often break, and the resultant flood waters inundate millions of acres of prime farmland. . . . Whenever the dikes break, hundreds of thousands of people are literally flooded out of house and home, and famine and pestilence [disease] are the usual results.

The Earliest Chinese Dynasty?

Despite the dangers of the river and the difficulties of taming it, early Chinese farmers and villagers persevered. Over time, population increased and villages grew into towns. Each town or district had a family or clan (a group of related families) that governed local life. It was only natural that local family lines of rulers, or dynasties, would develop.

According to tradition, the first dynasty that ruled over a large stretch of territory on the Yellow River was that of the Xia clan. The general date most often cited for the rise of the Xia state is ca. 2000 BC. This was about the time that Sumerian civilization was ebbing and giving way to its Babylonian and Assyrian offshoots.

There are serious questions about the Xia, however. Early Chinese literature mentions various Xia leaders and their exploits. However, little convincing archaeological evidence has been found to prove that these people and events were real. In 1959, excavators at the city of Yanshi, on the Luo River, a tributary of the Yellow, uncovered a large town with a building that looks like a palace. It dates from just after 2000 BC. Some scholars believe it is the ancient Xia capital, but this verdict has not been universally accepted.

Whether or not the Xia state ever actually existed, an agricultural civilization did thrive along the Yellow and Yangtze in that era. Existing evidence supports certain general conclusions about the local people and their culture. First, they were largely isolated from the other pockets of civilization that had grown up in Europe and other parts of Asia. This was because the Himalayas and other huge mountain ranges, along with deserts and other natural barriers, stood between the Chinese and the other peoples. So for a long while, few or no foreign cultural influences filtered into China.

Xia Dynasty bronze jue

The Entire Earthly Stage

As University of Washington scholar Patricia B. Ebrey points out here, the fact that China was long isolated from India, the Middle East, and Europe made the early Chinese see their region as the whole world.

To see the Chinese subcontinent as early Chinese saw it, we must erase from our minds all the maps we have seen showing it to occupy only a small fraction of the landmass of Eurasia, and far to one side at that. The Chinese subcontinent is so vast that by the first millennium BC the Chinese thought of it as All-Under-Heaven (*tianxia*), the entire earthly stage on which human beings acted out the drama of civilization. Surrounding it were vast oceans, wild deserts, steep mountains—regions much less central to the project of civilization. How far they extended, no one knew for sure. But the location of the center of civilization was not in doubt.

Also, archaeological evidence shows that life for most people in so-called Xia China was very difficult. Copper and bronze tools and weapons were in the process of replacing those of wood and stone. But metal-making processes were still primitive, so many people remained largely in the Stone Age. Most houses were primitive, too. They consisted of holes dug in the ground and covered over with tree branches and/or river reeds plastered with mud.

Rise of the Shang

The first Chinese dynasty and major kingdom that is well documented through archaeological evidence is that of the Shang. During late Xia times, in the 1700s BC, one of the many small agricultural communities or districts along the Yellow River began rising to prominence. It was centered at Zhengzhou, on the river's southern bank. (Later, the capital moved to Anyang, several miles north of the river.) Surviving literary sources indicate that a strong leader named Tang eventually emerged, perhaps in the 1600s BC. He overthrew the Xia and established a new dynasty known as the Shang.

The Shang, ruled by a king, dominated Chinese affairs in the North China Plain for some five centuries. It would be inaccurate to envision the Shang domain as a well-organized, stable kingdom. At the time, as many as two to three hundred small districts or sub-kingdoms existed along or near the river or its tributaries. Each may have consisted of an allied cluster of villages and towns similar to an Egyptian nome. These sub-kingdoms were known as guo, and they constantly vied for power among themselves. The Shang kingdom was only the most powerful of their number, and in order to maintain that status, the Shang rulers had to engage in almost relentless warfare.

For the thirty or so kings in the Shang dynasty, the key to victory in that warfare was the production of large numbers of bronze weapons. The smelting and manipulation of bronze (a mixture of copper and tin) became highly efficient under the Shang. Their soldiers utilized metal-tipped spears and arrows, long-handled axes with metal blades, and bronze helmets and armor. And these warriors were well organized into separate units with diverse skills. In addition to traditional infantry (foot soldiers), there were cavalry (warriors mounted on horses), archers, and charioteers. The Shang introduced chariots to China. (It is unknown whether the idea filtered in from India or farther west, or whether chariots developed

Bronze dagger-axe

One of the newly discovered pits of chariots and horses in the ruins of Yin, in central China's Henan province. Five of the seven pits are arranged in a line, with chariots and horses facing eastward. Yin was an ancient name for the Shang Dynasty.

independently in China.) Most of the other guo lacked the wealth and resources to produce chariots or masses of bronze weapons. So the Shang kings and nobles managed to hold sway in the region for a long time.

Shang Culture

These members of the Shang elite acquired many riches during their victories. Conquest also brought them many slaves, who toiled as laborers on building projects. The combination of wealth and cheap labor allowed the Shang leaders to create China's first large-scale, advanced culture. Outward signs of its success included huge defensive walls, palaces, and royal tombs. Zhengzhou's city walls were sixty feet wide, thirty feet high, and 2,385 feet long, for instance. Palaces were large structures constructed of wood, stone, and rammed earth (dirt packed so tightly it is almost as hard as stone). The royal tombs consisted of enormous pits strengthened by rammed earth and covered over by large timbers.

Graves of the Shang Nobles

J. A. G. Roberts, of England's University of Huddersfield, presents current evidence for how the Shang nobles were buried.

The Shang kings were buried in vast pits, which would have required the labor of many hundreds of men to excavate. Their corpses were placed in wooden coffins and these were surrounded by grave goods. On the ramps leading to the bottom of the pit lay human bodies and those of horses. The human victims, who may have been prisoners of war, had sometimes been beheaded. The main royal tombs at Anyang [the Shang capital] were robbed a very long time ago, but the tomb of Fu Hao, the consort [companion] of the Shang king who died c. 1250 BC, was discovered intact in 1976. It contained about two hundred bronze vessels, some in the shape of animals.

Another important aspect of the high culture that emerged under the Shang was China's first comprehensive writing system. "The Shang used a language directly ancestral to modern Chinese," Ebrey writes,

and moreover used a written script that evolved into the standard Chinese logographic writing system [in which a symbol or character represents a word] still in use today. Of the thousand-odd characters that have been deciphered, some are pictographs that visually represent a thing or an idea, some are borrowed for their sounds, and others are created by combining two characters, one giving meaning, the other sound. In China, as elsewhere, with writing comes list-making and efforts to organize thoughts that facilitate higher-order mental processes of abstraction and theorizing.

The Shang rulers also further developed and took full advantage of existing Chinese religious ideas in order to impose their authority. People believed in a number of deities and nature spirits, headed by a supreme god called Di. (An alternate theory suggests that Di was a collective term for all the gods.) But worship revolved mainly around the spirits of deceased ancestors. Ancestor worship, including the belief that the spirits of the dead have certain powers to affect the living for good or ill, was well-entrenched. (And it was destined to remain a fundamental part of Chinese religious systems for millennia to come.) It was thought that the departed ancestors, especially those of kings, communed with Di. Because the king was supposedly in contact with his ancestors, it was thought he had a direct channel to Di. That divine connection made the king more fit than anyone else to rule.

Western and Eastern Zhou

Though the Shang dynasts long reigned successfully, they were far from invincible. In about 1050 BC, Wu Wang, leader of one of the stronger Yellow River sub-kingdoms, overthrew the Shang leadership. Wu Wang became the first king of a new dynasty, the Zhou (or Chou). Modern scholars divide the long period of Zhou rule into two phases. Early, or Western, Zhou is dated from ca. 1050 to 771 BC; Late, or Eastern, Zhou is dated from 771 to 251 BC.

In order to rule the complex network of guo more efficiently, the early Zhou may have instituted a form of feudalism.

In this system, the king, or emperor, appointed trusted nobles to rule in outlying districts. Each feudal lord, or vassal, maintained control over the local peasants, most of whom were still farmers. He also owed allegiance to the king, who offered him favors and protection in return.

A passage from a Zhou literary text, the Book of Songs, lends some support for the existence of this feudal arrangement: "Everywhere under the vast heaven there is no land that is not the king's. To the borders of those lands there are none who are not the king's servants." Here, many scholars interpret "servants" as royal vassals (although a number of other scholars disagree and express doubt that the Zhou had a true feudal system).

In whatever manner the Zhou ruled, they introduced some important technical advances. Some were connected to agriculture and its practice within the Yellow's vast river system. One important improvement was the use of crop rotation—switching one's crops from one field to another every few years. This allowed the fallow, or unused, land to build up nutrients lost during repeated years of cultivation. The Zhou also introduced the raising of soy beans. These became a crucial new food source for both people and animals. In addition, tools and weapons made of iron, which is harder and more durable than bronze, appeared during Zhou times. The use of iron weapons helped the Zhou maintain their power.

Eventually, however, many other Chinese sub-kingdoms developed metal weaponry and challenged the Zhou for supremecy in the 800s and 700s BC. "They successfully attacked and sacked the Zhou's capital city," Wright says. "The Zhou government had to flee far to the east and set up another capital city, from which it ruled over a territory smaller than the original Zhou." This move marked the end of the Western Zhou and beginning of the Eastern Zhou.

The Eastern Zhou leaders never managed to maintain a state as strong and successful as the early members of the dynasty. Vassals of outlying districts in the shrinking Zhou

Fields on the banks of the Yellow River

domain increasingly ignored the commands of the king. And over time the Zhou kings became mainly figureheads. In 221 BC, a new dynasty, the Qin (or Chin), overcame and replaced the Zhou.

It was the Qin who finally unified most of the far-flung, bickering Chinese kingdoms into a single, centralized state ruled by an emperor. Some version of that state was destined to last into modern times. The original civilization that had grown up along the Yellow and Yangtze rivers survived, in one form or another, to the present. As great as they were, the cultures of ancient Mesopotamia and Egypt vanished long ago. But China endures.

Chapter Six:
The Indus Valley Civilization

Not too long ago, archaeologists and historians regularly spoke about the world's three cradles of civilization. As late as 1920 the common wisdom was that Mesopotamia, Egypt, and China had given rise to the first advanced cultures. All three civilizations had grown up along major rivers. And in the fertile soils of these river valleys, the first cities, nations, large irrigation projects, and writing systems had taken firm root. No one suspected that a fourth great river civilization lay buried beneath the surface of modern-day India.

In retrospect, it seems odd that historians and archaeologists ignored the signs of India's cradle of civilization. One sign was geographical in nature. Across the northern tier of India stretches the world's mightiest cluster of mountain peaks—the Himalayas. It and other nearby mountain ranges contain numerous glaciers and massive snow-packs. Each spring, run-off from these sources flows southward and feeds an enormous river plain and valley that covers hundreds of thousands of square miles. Through this vast, fertile region flow three major rivers—the Indus, the Ganges, and the Brahmaputra.

Along with their many tributaries, they form a lush and fruitful expanse of territory exceedingly suited to farming and settlement.

Other signs consisted of the remains of humans and their works in that huge river valley. Evidence, including stone tools, showed that primitive hunter-gatherers had entered India from the west at least by 200,000 BC and likely considerably earlier. An unusually large number of these tools were found in the Punjab region. (That expanse, containing several rivers that flow into the Indus, is along the border with modern-day Pakistan, which used to be part of India. And most of the Indus River system is now in Pakistan.) Permanent settlements began developing in the area between 7000 and 6000 BC. And archaeologists proposed that knowledge of agriculture had begun to filter into India from the Middle East.

All of the preconditions needed for the rise of a great river civilization existed in northern India. Why no one purposely searched for it is a mystery. But when modern excavators finally did unearth its remains, they realized the significance of their discovery. John Keay, a noted historian and writer, recalls:

> It was pure chance that Indian and British archaeologists, while investigating [ancient ruins] at Mohenjo-daro in [the] Sind [region] and at Harappa in the Punjab made the prehistoric discovery of the twentieth century. They called their find the 'Indus valley civilization,' and drew the obvious comparisons with those of Egypt and Sumeria. Indeed, they thought it might be an offshoot of the latter. Later, as its sophisticated and surprisingly uniform culture became more apparent, the Indus valley civilization was accorded distinct status. And when the extent of its cultural reach was found to embrace a host of other sites, many of them well beyond

View of the Himalayas from the Ganges River

The ruins of Harappa, in Pakistan

the valley of the Indus, it was renamed after one
of those sites as the Harappan civilization.

The First Known City-Planners

The chief remains of the once vast and mighty Harappan river
civilization consist of the ruins of large towns and cities. The
ruins are scattered over an area of roughly 1.5 million square
miles (3.9 million sq. km). This is twice the size of the territory controlled by the Egyptian pharaohs who erected the
pyramids at Giza.

The two most famous Harappan city-sites—at Harappa
and Mohenjo-daro (meaning "Mound of the Dead")—date
from 2600 BC. At that time or somewhat later, Harappa was
at least 3 miles (4.8 km) in circumference and had a population of 35,000 to 40,000 people. That is comparable to most of
the Mesopotamian cities of the same period. However, cities
of that size or close to it had already existed in the Tigris-
Euphrates valley for several centuries when the Harrapan
cities arose. So Mesopotamia still retains the distinction of
producing the world's first cities.

Nevertheless, the Indus Valley Civilization claims a rather
significant distinction of its own: its inhabitants built the
world's first pre-planned towns and cities. The early cities of
Mesopotamia and China (and later those of ancient Europe)
grew organically—they began as small villages. People kept
adding new sections as needed, usually basing new streets on
existing footpaths. As a result, the layout of streets, houses,
and shops tended to be chaotic, jumbled, and quite often
inefficient. In contrast, most of the Harappan cities featured
layouts that were planned in advance, making them orderly
and efficient. Tarini Carr, an anthropologist, describes this
earliest known example of city planning, as well as some of
the advanced plumbing and other innovations the Harappan
builders incorporated:

Harappa, along with the other Indus Valley cities, had a level of architectural planning that was
unparalleled in the ancient world. The city was
laid out in a grid-like pattern with the orientation
of streets and buildings according to the cardi-
nal directions [north, south, east, and west]. To
facilitate the access to other neighborhoods and
to segregate private and public areas, the city and
streets were particularly organized. The city had
many drinking water wells, and a highly sophisticated system of waste removal. All Harappan
houses were equipped with latrines, bathing
houses, and sewage drains which emptied into
larger mains and eventually deposited the fertile
sludge on surrounding agricultural fields. It has
been surprising to archaeologists that the site
layouts and artifact styles throughout the Indus
region are very similar. It has been concluded
these indicate that there was uniform economic
and social structure within these cities.

Almost all of the buildings, walls, wells, drains, and other
structures in the Indus valley communities were made of brick.
It was not that the builders were unfamiliar or uncomfortable
with wood and stone construction. Rather, Keay points out,
"four thousand years ago stone was as scarce in the lower Indus
region as it is today." He adds:

Even the local timber, though more plentiful than
now . . . seems not to have been sufficiently well-
grown for major construction purposes. Instead,
it was used as fuel to fire brick kilns. The
Harappans built almost entirely in brick, both
sun-baked and kiln-fired, and the excellence of
their firing is well attested by the survival . . .
of so many [of their] structures. . . . Brick work,

however, has its limitations. [Sun], salt, and wind play havoc with a mortar of mud; weight stresses cause bowing and buckling. [So] few if any buildings at Mohenjo-daro were of more than two stories. Even supposing the Harappans had aspired to the monumental extravagances of their Egyptian contemporaries, it is hard to see how they could have achieved them.

Standardized Construction

Almost all of the Harappans' structures were composed of bricks. They created these bricks by pouring clay into wooden molds. The proto-bricks were removed from the molds while still moist. Then the brick-makers either left them out in the sun to dry or baked them in stone-lined kilns. The resulting bricks looked extremely similar to modern ones—when modern excavators first dug at Mohenjo-daro, the bricks they found made them think that the city's buildings were less than a century old. The Harappan bricks were also of a standardized size, as pointed out by Carr:

> It would seem that a standard brick size was developed and used throughout the Indus cities. Besides similar brick size standard weights are seen to have been used throughout the region as well. The weights that have been recovered have shown a remarkable accuracy. They follow a binary decimal system: 1, 2, 4, 8, 16, 32, up to 12,800 units, where one unit weighs approximately 0.85 grams.

Trade and Prosperity

The Harappan towns and cities enjoyed a great deal of prosperity for several centuries. Evidence suggests that their influence, wealth, and power peaked between about 2600 and 1900 BC. The political arrangement of these settlements in that period is still uncertain. Some scholars used to assume they were all part of a single nation or empire, but most now doubt that was the case. It appears instead that the Harappan cities were mainly independent and that they were linked mainly by language and culture. Historian Gordon Johnson points to studies of the largest Harappan city, Mohenjo-daro. It "does not appear to have exercised imperial power over" the other Harappan sites, he writes, although "it probably formed some sort of administrative center."

Whatever the political status of these cities may have been, there is no doubt that they engaged in extensive trade. Some of that trade was likely land-based. But the most far-ranging and lucrative traders took advantage of the Indus and its connection with the sea. Harappan merchant ships, built of wood, traveled down the river and entered the Indian Ocean. The full extent of their destinations and contacts remains unknown. But at least some of the vessels sailed westward and into the Persian Gulf.

Along the Persian Gulf's northwestern shores were a number of prosperous Sumerian cities, including Ur and Larsa. At these busy ports, the Sumerians welcomed foreign traders, who are mentioned in several ancient Mesopotamian documents. Some scholars think that a word that appears frequently in these documents—Meluhha—was Sumerian for "Harappan." The Sumerians offered some of their own goods to the Harappans. In exchange, the visiting merchants from faraway India offered their own copper, gold, grain, timber, and ivory. Particularly coveted by the Sumerians was Harappan cotton cloth. Some sources believe that the residents of the

Burial urn (circa 2000 BC) from the Harappan civilization

Indus valley were the first people in the world to spin cotton yarn into cloth.

Commercial interactions between these two great river civilizations were frequent and continued for years. Proof for this long-lasting relationship takes the form of Harrapan seals, many of which have been found in the ruins of Mesopotamian cities. The seals were small disks. Each was made of baked clay and had some word-symbols and one or more little pictures carved or stamped onto it. Typical images were of animals, gods, and various common objects.

Thousands of such seals have also been found in the Harappan towns and cities. Some evidence suggests that the locals used them in everyday commercial exchanges such as the buying and selling of goods. According to Keay, the seals appear to have been

> carried about or worn, each having a boss or hole by which they could be threaded on a string. The [wide] distribution of the seals suggests that [they] may have been used to facilitate the exchange of goods over long distances. [The] stamped image, attached to a consignment of goods, might have identified their owner . . . destination or contents, and so have served somewhat the role of a bill or even a bar-code. Clearly, if this was indeed their purpose, their multiplicity and far-flung distribution argues for a vast and buzzing commercial network.

The vast natural resources of the Indus valley and the stable, ordered life of the Harappan cities complemented such lucrative trade, both local and long-distance. Together, these elements created substantial wealth and prosperity. And as historian Sinharaja Tammita-Delgoda points out, this must have translated into a high standard of living for a large portion of the population. "This was a society," he says, "which could even afford to provide for the needs of its poorest and most lowly elements, even the workers or slaves. In many cases, they were far better housed than the average Indian laborer is today. The prosperity of this world rested on its stability. Order was far more important than change."

The Fate of Civilizations

However, as eventually happens to all civilizations, even the most successful ones, that of the Harappans declined and gave way to others. The decline, which was slow but steady, began around 1900 BC. One cause appears to have been a gradual dwindling of long-range trade, which had long been a vital source of wealth. Also, houses and other buildings in the cities fell into disrepair, and fewer and fewer were repaired over time. Finally, as the centuries wore on, many of these settlements were completely abandoned. Most of the surviving residents appear to have migrated away from the central sector of the Indus valley.

For much of the twentieth century, most historians thought that the Harappan decline was caused by an invasion of a people from the west. These alleged invaders became known as the Aryans. However, a great deal of recent evidence has called that theory into question. A majority of scholars now think that major climatic and environmental changes were the chief cause of the demise of the Indus valley civilization. Over time, these brought about sharp economic decline and widespread poverty. Studies reveal that extensive sections of the central Indus plain became very arid in the early second millennium BC. This badly damaged agriculture in the region. And combined with the ongoing loss of trade, economic collapse was inevitable.

By 1700–1600 BC, most of the Harappan sites had become deserted. But the Harappans were not all dead. Many had simply reverted to small-scale rural farming and a more backward culture.

The ancient ruins of Mohenjo-daro, one of the largest cities of the Indus valley civilization, in Pakistan

The Harappan Decline

Noted Indian archaeologist B. B. Lal summarizes the latest consensus for why Harappan civilization declined. He is careful to make the point that not all of the Harappans disappeared, which used to be the prevailing hypothesis:

Over-exploitation and consequent wearing out of the landscape must have led to a fall in agricultural production. Added to it was probably a change in the climate towards aridity. And no less significant was a marked fall in trade, both internal as well as external. As a result of all this, there was no longer the affluence that used to characterize this civilization. The cities began to disappear and there was a reversion to a rural scenario. [There] was no doubt a setback in the standards of living but no extinction of the culture itself.

Soon, invigorated by new technical and cultural ideas filtering in from the west, the inhabitants of the region would rise again to new prosperity. In fact, current scholarship suggests that the Aryans, now called the Vedic culture, who replaced the Harappans in the area, were not outside invaders. It appears instead that the Vedic culture developed directly out of the remnants of Harappan culture. The majestic river civilization of the Indus gave life to new generations who would owe their existence to its life-giving waters. As in the other cradles of humanity—centered on the Tigris-Euphrates, Nile, and Yellow—the river would remain. Trusted and seemingly eternal, it would continue to provide for those who dwelled along its fertile banks.

The remains of a Harappan town, part of the Indus valley civilization, which thrived from about 3000 to 1700 BC

The Great Wall of China, and the Yellow River in the Tengger desert at Shapotou near Zhongwei, Ningxia Province, China

✹ Timeline
BC

ca. 9000	Agriculture begins in Fertile Crescent region of Mesopotamia.
ca. 5500	Inhabitants of Fertile Crescent migrate to Tigris-Euphrates river valley.
ca. 4000	Egyptian farmers exploit yearly floods of Nile River for irrigation.
ca. 3500-3000	Sumerians build world's first cities on plains northwest of Persian Gulf.
ca. 3100	Egypt's two kingdoms, the Red and White Lands, unite and become world's first nation-state.
ca. 2600	Cities of Harappa and Mohenjo-daro emerge in India's Indus river valley.
ca. 2686	Beginning of Egypt's Old Kingdom; great pyramids at Giza are erected.
ca. 2589	Khufu, builder of Great Pyramid at Giza, ascends Egypt's throne.
ca. 2300	Sargon, a Mesopotamian, establishes world's first empire.
ca. 2181	End of Egypt's Old Kingdom.
ca. 2000	Rise of the Xia, China's first dynasty.
ca. 1900	India's Harappan cities begin to decline.
ca. 1600	Shang dynasty assumes power in China's Yellow River plain.
ca. 1150	Zhou dynasty overcomes the Shang.
ca. 251	Zhou rulers give way to the Qin dynasty.

✿ Sources

CHAPTER ONE:
The Land Between the Rivers

p. 11, "Rivers must have been the guides . . ." Henry David Thoreau, *A Week on the Concord and Merrimack Rivers*; Walden, or, *Life in the Woods; The Maine Woods; Cape Cod* (New York: Library of America, 1985), 12–13.

p. 13-14, "People may have perceived . . ." Daniel C. Snell, *Life in the Ancient Near East, 3100–332 B.C.E.* (New Haven: Yale University Press, 1997), 14.

p. 14, "The Agricultural Revolution . . ." L. Sprague de Camp, *Great Cities of the Ancient World* (New York: Barnes and Noble, 1972), 7–8.

p. 15, "Once the feasibility of growing crops . . ." W. H. McNeill, *The Rise of the West: A History of the Human Community* (Chicago: University of Chicago Press, 1963), 46–48.

p. 16, "By the close of the Ubaid[ian] period . . ." Norman B. Hunt, *Historical Atlas of Ancient Mesopotamia* (New York: Facts On File / Thalamus Publishing, 2004), 15.

p. 19, 22, "Each city proper was girdled . . ." Chester G. Starr, *A History of the Ancient World* (New York: Oxford University Press, 1991), 32–33.

p. 22, "In a year of low floods . . ." McNeill, *The Rise of the West,* 48.

p. 23, "eager to control as much as possible . . ." Samuel N. Kramer, *Cradle of Civilization* (New York: Time-Life, 1967), 34.

CHAPTER TWO:
Life in the First Cities

p. 26, "While the physical image . . ." Kramer, *Cradle of Civilization,* 79.

p. 26-27, "crowded with houses . . ." Karen R. Nemet-Nejat, *Daily Life in Ancient Mesopotamia* (Peabody, MA: Hendrickson, 1998), 103–105.

p. 27, "If a builder builds a house . . ." Richard Hooker, "The Code of Hammurabi," http://www.wsu.edu/~dee/MESO/CODE.HTM.

p. 28, "A comfortable home made of brick . . ." Stephen Bertman, *Handbook to Life in Ancient Mesopotamia* (New York: Facts On File, 2003), 287.

p. 29, "A tiled drain . . ." Ibid.

p. 31, "Food was prepared in an oven . . ." Nemet-Nejat, *Daily Life in Ancient Mesopotamia,* 126.

p. 32, "Meat is not needed . . ." John Lawton, "Mesopotamian Menus," Saudi Aramco World (March/April 1988), http://www.saudiaramcoworld. com/ issue/198802/mesopotamian.menus.htm.

p. 33, "If a woman quarrel with her husband . . ." Hooker, "The Code of Hammurabi."

p. 33, "Because communication within cities . . ." Gwendolyn Leick, *The Babylonians* (New York: Routledge, 2003), 84.

p. 35, "The merchant who [practices] trickery . . ." Ibid., 84–85.

CHAPTER THREE:
The Gift of the River

p. 40, "bread, cakes . . ." Fekri Hassan, "The Gift of the Nile," in *Ancient Egypt,* ed. David P. Silverman (New York: Oxford University Press, 1997), 12–13.

p. 40, "The rains fall every year . . ." Rosalie David, *Handbook to Life in Ancient Egypt* (New York: Oxford University Press, 1998), 64.

p. 41, "the gift of the river . . ." Herodotus, *Histories,* trans. Aubrey de Sélincourt (New York: Penguin, 1972), 131.

p. 41, "He waters the landscape . . ." John L. Foster, trans., *Ancient Egyptian Literature* (Austin: University of Texas Press, 2001), 111–113.

p. 43, "The main image on the palette . . ." Rita Freed, "Predynastic and Early Dynastic Art" in Silverman, *Ancient Egypt,* 215.

p. 45, "Religion permeated an Egyptian's total existence . . ." Lionel Casson, *Everyday Life in Ancient Egypt* (Baltimore: Johns Hopkins University Press, 2001), 79.

p. 45, "We of the West . . ." Ibid.

p. 49, "was employed at the temple . . ." Ian Shaw and Paul Nicholson, *The Dictionary of Ancient Egypt* (New York: Harry N. Abrams, 1995), 228.

p. 49, "The priests shave their bodies . . ." Herodotus, *Histories,* 143.

CHAPTER FOUR:
Builders of the Pyramids

p. 53-54, "The pyramids are . . . more than mere wonders . . ." Desmond Stewart, *The Pyramids and the Sphinx* (New York: Newsweek, 1971), 18.

p. 55, "The superstructure was rectangular . . ." David, *Handbook to Life in Ancient Egypt,* 144–146.

p. 57, "He [the pharaoh] rushes at the sky . . ." Josephine Mayer and Tom Prideaux, ed., *Never to Die: The Egyptians in Their Own Words* (New York: Viking, 1938), 42–43.

p. 58, "The mortuary temple was the focus . . ." Stewart, *The Pyramids and the Sphinx,* 41.

p. 60, "The core of Khufu's pyramid . . ." Jill Kamil, *The Ancient Egyptians: Life in the Old Kingdom* (Cairo: American University in Cairo Press, 1996), 80.

p. 61, "brought the country into all sorts of misery . . ." Herodotus, *Histories,* 178.

p. 62, "The mason cutting with his chisel . . ." Foster, *Ancient Egyptian Literature,* 34.

p. 63, "We found a large Old Kingdom settlement . . ." Zahi Hawass, "The Discovery of the Tombs of the Pyramid Builders at Giza," Guardian's Egypt, www.guardians.net/hawass/buildtomb.htm.

p. 66, "One of the statuettes depicts . . ." Ibid.

CHAPTER FIVE:
A Blessing and a Curse

p. 69, "The Yellow River is both a blessing and a curse . . ." David. C. Wright, *The History of China* (Westport, CT: Greenwood Press, 2001), 3.

p. 71, "To see the Chinese subcontinent . . ." Patricia B. Ebrey, *Cambridge Illustrated History of China* (New York: Cambridge University Press, 2003), 13.

p. 75, "The Shang kings were buried in vast pits . . ." J. A. G. Roberts, *A Concise History of China* (Cambridge, MA: Harvard University Press, 1999), 6.

p. 75-76, "The Shang used a language . . ." Ebrey, *Cambridge Illustrated History of China,* 27.

p. 77, "Everywhere under the vast heaven . . ." Roberts, *A Concise History of China,* 9.

p. 77, "They successfully attacked . . ." Wright, *The History of China,* 20.

CHAPTER SIX:
The Indus Valley Civilization

p. 82, 85, "It was pure chance . . ." John Keay, *India: A History* (New York: Grove, 2000), 5.

p. 86, "Harappa, along with the other Indus Valley cities . . ." Tarini J. Carr, "The Harappan Civilization," Archaeology Online, http://www.archaeologyonline.net/artifacts/harappa-mohenjodaro.html.

p. 86-87, "Four thousand years ago . . ." Keay, *India: A History,* 8.

p. 87, "It would seem that a standard brick size . . ." Carr, "The Harappan Civilization."

p. 88, "does not appear to have exercised . . ." Gordon Johnson, *Cultural Atlas of India* (New York: Facts on File, 1996), 62.

p. 90, "carried about or worn . . ." Keay, *India: A History,* 16.

p. 90-91, "This was a society which could even afford . . ." Sinharaja Tammita-Delgoda, *A Traveller's History of India* (New York: Interlink, 1999), 31–32.

p. 94, "Over-exploitation and consequent wearing out of the landscape . . ." B. B. Lal, "Why Perpetuate Myths? A Fresh Look at Indian History," The Cycle of Time, http://www.cycleoftime.com/articles_view.php?Cod Artigo=54.

✿ Bibliography

Selected Books

Ascalone, Enrico. *Mesopotamia: Assyrians, Sumerians, Babylonians.* Berkeley: University of California Press, 2007.

Bertman, Stephen. *Handbook to Life in Ancient Mesopotamia.* New York: Facts on File, 2003.

Ebrey, Patricia B. *Cambridge Illustrated History of China.* New York: Cambridge University Press, 2003.

Edwards, I. E. S. *The Pyramids of Egypt.* New York: Penguin, 1993.

Freed, Rita. "Predynastic and Early Dynastic Art," in *Ancient Egypt,* edited by David P. Silverman. New York: Oxford University Press, 1997.

Gernet, Jacques. *A History of Chinese Civilization.* Cambridge: Cambridge University Press, 1996.

Grimal, Nicolas. *A History of Ancient Egypt.* Translated by Ian Shaw. Oxford, England: Blackwell, 1992.

Hassan, Fekri. "The Gift of the Nile," in *Ancient Egypt,* edited by David P. Silverman. New York: Oxford University Press, 1997.

Hunt, Norman B. *Historical Atlas of Ancient Mesopotamia.* New York: Facts on File / Thalamus Publishing, 2004.

Kamil, Jill. *The Ancient Egyptians: Life in the Old Kingdom.* Cairo: American University in Cairo Press, 1996.

Keay, John. *India: A History.* New York: Grove, 2000.

Leick, Gwendolyn. *The Babylonians.* London: Routledge, 2003.

Lehner, Mark. *The Complete Pyramids.* London: Thames and Hudson, 1997.

Lloyd, Seton. *The Archaeology of Mesopotamia.* London: Thames and Hudson, 1985.

————. *Foundations in the Dust: A Story of Mesopotamian Exploration.* New York: Thames and Hudson, 1981.

Luckenbill, Daniel D., ed. *Ancient Records of Assyria and Babylonia. 2 vols.* New York: Greenwood Press, 1989.

Meyers, E. M., ed. *The Oxford Encyclopedia of Archaeology in the Near East. 5 vols.* New York: Oxford University Press, 1997.

Nemet-Nejat, Karen R. *Daily Life in Ancient Mesopotamia.* Peabody, MA: Hendrickson, 1998.

Possehl, Gregory L. *Harappan Civilization.* Oxford: IBH, 1993.

Pritchard, James B., ed. *Ancient Near Eastern Texts Relating to the Old Testament.* Princeton: Princeton University Press, 1969.

Reisner, George. *The Development of the Egyptian Tomb Down to the Accession of Cheops.* Brockton, MA: Pye Rare Books, 1996.

Roberts, J. A. G. *A Concise History of China.* Cambridge, MA: Harvard University Press, 1999.

Shaw, Ian, ed. *The Oxford History of Ancient Egypt.* Oxford, England: Oxford University Press, 2000.

Silverman, David P., ed. *Ancient Egypt.* New York: Oxford University Press, 1997.

Stein, Burton. *A History of India.* Oxford, England: Blackwell, 1998.

Wright, David. C. *The History of China.* Westport, CT: Greenwood Press, 2001.

Web Sites

Ancient China
www.crystalinks.com/china.html

Ancient Egypt
www.ancient-egypt.org

Ancient Mesopotamia: Archaeology
http://oi.uchicago.edu/OI/MUS/ED/TRC/MESO/archae-
ology.html

Building in Ancient Egypt
www.reshafim.org.il/ad/egypt/building

Hammurabi
www.humanistictexts.org/hammurabi.htm

The Indus Civilization
http://www.harappa.com/har/har0.html

The Pyramids: The Inside Story
www.pbs.org/wgh/nova/pyramid

✥ Glossary

barter system: Paying for something with an object of equal value.

bronze: A metal made by mixing copper and tin.

casing stones: The smooth limestone blocks that originally formed the outside surfaces of Egypt's great pyramids.

cavalry: Soldiers mounted on horses.

clan: A group of related families.

cult image: A statue of a god, usually resting inside a temple.

cuneiform: A system of writing that developed in ancient Mesopotamia, featuring small wedged-shaped characters.

dowry: In many cultures around the world, money or valuables supplied by a bride's father for her maintenance in her marriage.

dynasty: A family line of rulers.

guo: In ancient China, small districts, each consisting of an allied group of villages and towns.

inundation: In ancient Egypt, the yearly flooding of the Nile River.

infantry: Foot soldiers.

karum: In ancient Mesopotamia, a commercial district or group of merchants.

loess: In China, the rich soil deposited by the Yellow River.

mastaba: In ancient Egypt, a low, rectangular tomb made of mud bricks or stone.

ma'at: In ancient Egypt, a state of order and harmony.

me (parsu in Babylonia): In ancient Sumeria, divine rules guiding nature and human affairs.

millet: A nutritious grain that grows well in semi-arid regions.

mortuary temple: In ancient Egypt, a temple built to maintain a deceased pharaoh's spirit in the afterlife.

nome: In ancient Egypt, a small political unit consisting of an allied group of villages.

patriarchal: Male-dominated.

procession: A parade, often religious in nature.

rammed earth: Dirt that has been compacted until it is almost as hard as stone.

relief (or bas-relief): A carved scene raised somewhat from a flat surface.

seal: A small token made of baked clay, with words and/or pictures carved or stamped on it.

scribe: In the ancient world, a person who used his or her reading and writing skills in some professional capacity.

sphinx: In ancient Egypt, a mythical creature combining the features of a human and a lion; or a statue of such a creature.

urban center: A city.

vassal: A local ruler who owes allegiance to a king or emperor.

vizier: In ancient Egypt, the king's chief administrator.

ziggurat: In ancient Mesopotamia, a large, pyramid-like structure having religious significance.

✲ Index

꧁ Picture Credits

Cover, 6-7: © North Wind Picture Archives / Alamy

12:	Used under license from iStockphoto.com
18:	Used under license from iStockphoto.com
20:	ALI JAREKJI/Reuters /Landov
23:	Ivy Close Images /Landov
28:	Used under license from iStockphoto.com
30:	Courtesy of the Library of Congress
31:	Used under license from iStockphoto.com
34:	Used under license from iStockphoto.com
35:	Used under license from iStockphoto.com
37:	Used under license from iStockphoto.com
38:	Courtesy of ASP GeoImaging/NASA
44:	ancientnile/Alamy
47:	Used under license from iStockphoto.com
48:	Used under license from iStockphoto.com
50:	Used under license from iStockphoto.com
54:	Used under license from iStockphoto.com
56:	Used under license from iStockphoto.com
59:	Used under license from iStockphoto.com
62:	Interfoto/Alamy
64:	Used under license from iStockphoto.com
68:	Courtesy of Andre Holdrinet
70:	Private collection
73:	Private collection
74:	Reuters /Landov
78:	Robert Harding Picture Library Ltd/Alamy
83:	Used under license from iStockphoto.com
84:	Robert Harding Picture Library Ltd/Alamy
89:	Anders Blonquist/Alamy
92:	Courtesy of M. Imran
95:	© Mike Goldwater /Alamy
96:	© Mike Goldwater /Alamy

ROOSEVELT PUBLIC LIBRARY
27 WEST FULTON AVENUE
ROOSEVELT NY 11575
516-378-0222
01/10/2012